TIME FOR KIDS

Amazon Rainforest

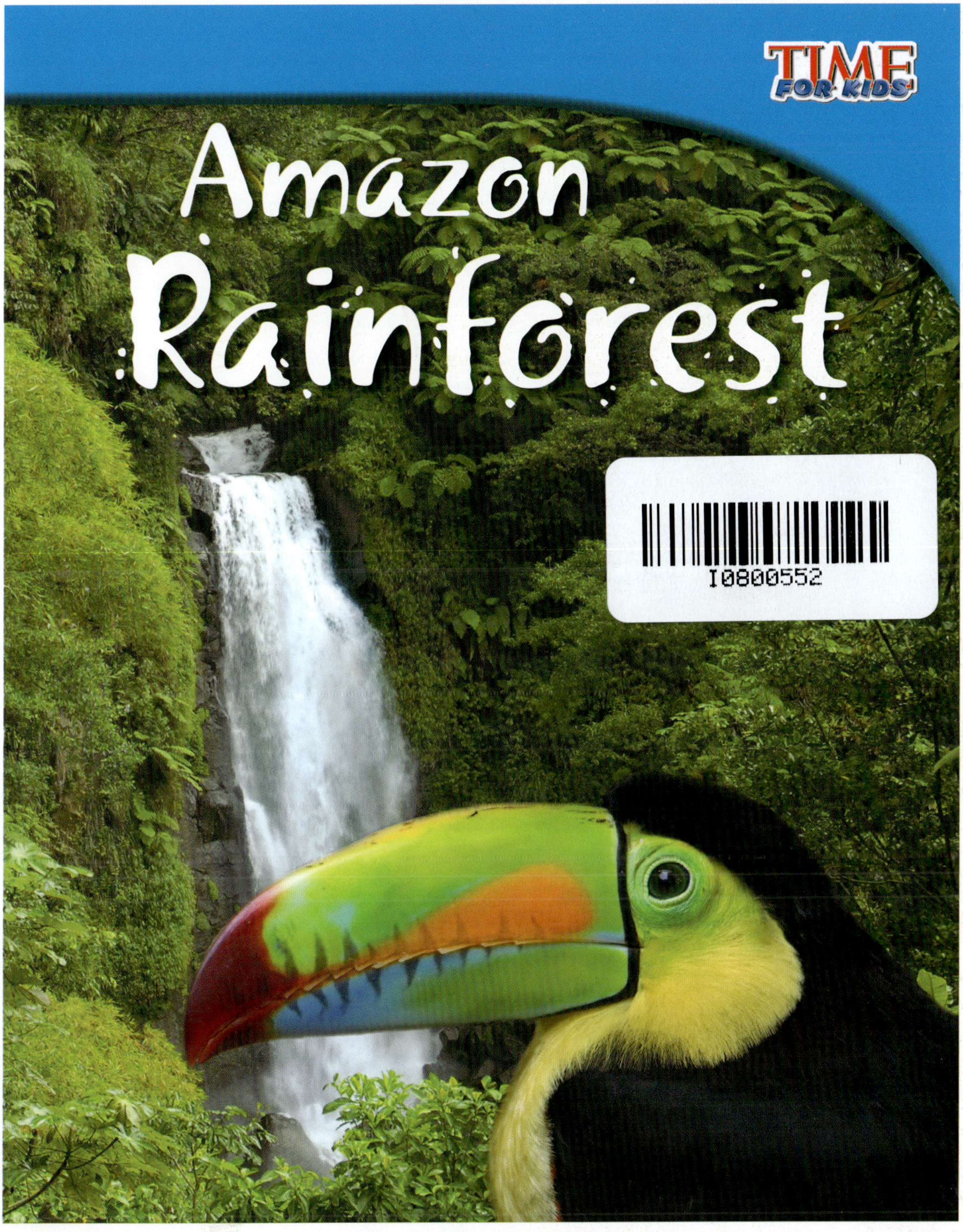

William B. Rice

Consultant

Timothy Rasinski, Ph.D.
Kent State University

Publishing Credits

Dona Herweck Rice, *Editor-in-Chief*
Robin Erickson, *Production Director*
Lee Aucoin, *Creative Director*
Conni Medina, M.A.Ed., *Editorial Director*
Jamey Acosta, *Editor*
Heidi Kellenberger, *Editor*
Lexa Hoang, *Designer*
Stephanie Reid, *Photo Editor*
Rachelle Cracchiolo, M.S.Ed., *Publisher*

Image Credits

Cover Erkki & Hanna/Shutterstock; inset: Braam Collins/Shutterstock; p.2-3 Paul Aniszewski/Shutterstock; p.3 Andrea Haase/Shutterstock; p.4-5 Paul Aniszewski/Shutterstock; p.5 top to bottom: A Cotton Photo/Shutterstock; Jim Agronick/Shutterstock; p.6-7 Andrey.tiyk/Shutterstock; p.7 top to bottom: Eky Studio/Shutterstock; Hal_P/Shutterstock; antart/Shutterstock; p.8-9 2009fotofriends/Shutterstock; p.9 top to bottom: 2009fotofriends/Shuttertstock; Eric Baker/Shutterstock; p.10-11 Dr. Morley Read/ Shutterstock; p.10 Eric Gevaert/ Shutterstock; p.11 top to bottom: AridOcean/Shutterstock; Johnny Lye/ Shutterstock; p.12-13 guentermanaus/Shutterstock; p.12 Universal Images Group/Getty Images; p.13 ecoventurestravel/Shutterstock; p.14-15 guentermanaus/Shutterstock; p.14 top to bottom: Ammit/ Shutterstock; Frontpage/ Shutterstock; p.15 rsfatt/Shutterstock; p.16-17 Leagam/Shutterstock; p.16 top to bottom: generacionx/iStockphoto; windmoon/Shutterstock; p.17 amathers/iStockphoto; p.18-19 Dr. Morley Read/Shutterstock; p.18 top to bottom: Gordon Wiltsie/National Geographic Stock; Dirk Ercken/Shutterstock; p.19 Dr. Morley Read/ Shuttetstock; p.20-21 Dr. Morley Read/Shutterstock; p.21 top to bottom: Andrea Haase/Shutterstock; p.22-23 Ronnie Howard/Shutterstock; p.22 dstephens/ iStockphoto; p.24-25 Berndt Fischer/Photolibrary; p.25 E. Sweet/Shutterstock; p.26-27 Dr. Morley Read/ Shutterstock; p.26 Eric Isselée/Shuttetrstock; p.27 top: Eduardo Rivero/Shutterstock; p.27 bottom: Ivanova Inga/Shutterstock; p.28-29 Sergey Kamshylin/Shutterstock; p.28 Shi Yali/Shutterstock; p.29 luoman/ iStockphoto; p.30-31 Paul Aniszewski/Shutterstock; p.32 Dr. Morley Read/ Shutterstock; back cover: windmoon/Shutterstock

Based on writing from *TIME For Kids.*

Teacher Created Materials
5301 Oceanus Drive
Huntington Beach, CA 92649-1030
http://www.tcmpub.com

ISBN 978-1-4333-3671-3

Printed by: 590835
Printed in: Taiwan

Table of Contents

Ancient Forests

Forests have been around for a long time. They were here on Earth before people were. Forests cover huge areas of land. They cross many, many miles.

Forests may be the most beautiful places on Earth. There is so much to see, smell, and hear there. Trees grow thick and tall. Animals are in the trees and on the ground.

Tropical rainforests may be the most beautiful forests of all. This book is about the largest tropical rainforest in the world, the Amazon.

Kelp beds are like underwater forests.

What Makes a Forest?

Forests are places where many trees and plants grow thickly across a large area of land. Of course, trees and plants grow all over. But they do not always make a forest. It takes many trees and plants growing close together to make a forest.

Trees are a key part of forests. It does not matter what type of trees they are. Different trees and plants like to grow in different settings. Some trees and plants grow where it is hot and dry, as in deserts. Some trees and plants grow where it is wet and cold, as in mountains. Some grow where it is rainy and hot most of the year. Those are tropical rainforests.

About Trees

Trees are woody plants with a single main stem or trunk and many branches. Most experts define trees as being at least 10 feet tall and alive for many years. This diagram shows the main parts of a tree.

Tropical rainforests are exactly as they sound. They are rainy and wet. Some can get over six feet of rain each year!

The tropics are the area around the middle of Earth. So, rainforests there are tropical rainforests. Another word for them is *jungle*.

Temperate Rainforest

The Hoh Rainforest is found in the northwest United States. It is a **temperate rainforest**. A rainforest is called *temperate* when it is located within the temperate zones on Earth, and it is usually cooler than the tropics. The Hoh can get over 150 inches of rain each year.

Hoh Rainforest, Olympic National Park

Amazon Rainforest

One of the greatest rainforests in the world is the Amazon rainforest. It is in the northern half of South America. It is often just called *the Amazon*. The Amazon is known around the world.

The Amazon is huge. It crosses many countries. The biggest part is in Brazil. It covers about half of Brazil!

There are many kinds of plants and animals in the Amazon. There are more kinds there than anywhere else in the world. They have plenty of water because there is a lot of rain.

The emperor tamarin is one of the many animals that live in the Amazon.

The Amazon

The Amazon Rainforest covers 1.4 billion acres! An acre is just a little smaller than a soccer field or a football field.

There are many big rivers and streams in the Amazon, too. All of them flow to the Amazon River. It is the biggest river on Earth. It has more water in it than any other river. It is so big that it breaks into many **stems**. The stems are as large as normal-sized rivers. All the stems flow to the ocean.

Amazon water is **freshwater**. That means it does not have much salt in it. It is the kind of water that people drink. Water in the ocean is **saltwater**. It has a lot of salt. So much water from the Amazon goes into the ocean that it is still freshwater about 100 miles out to sea!

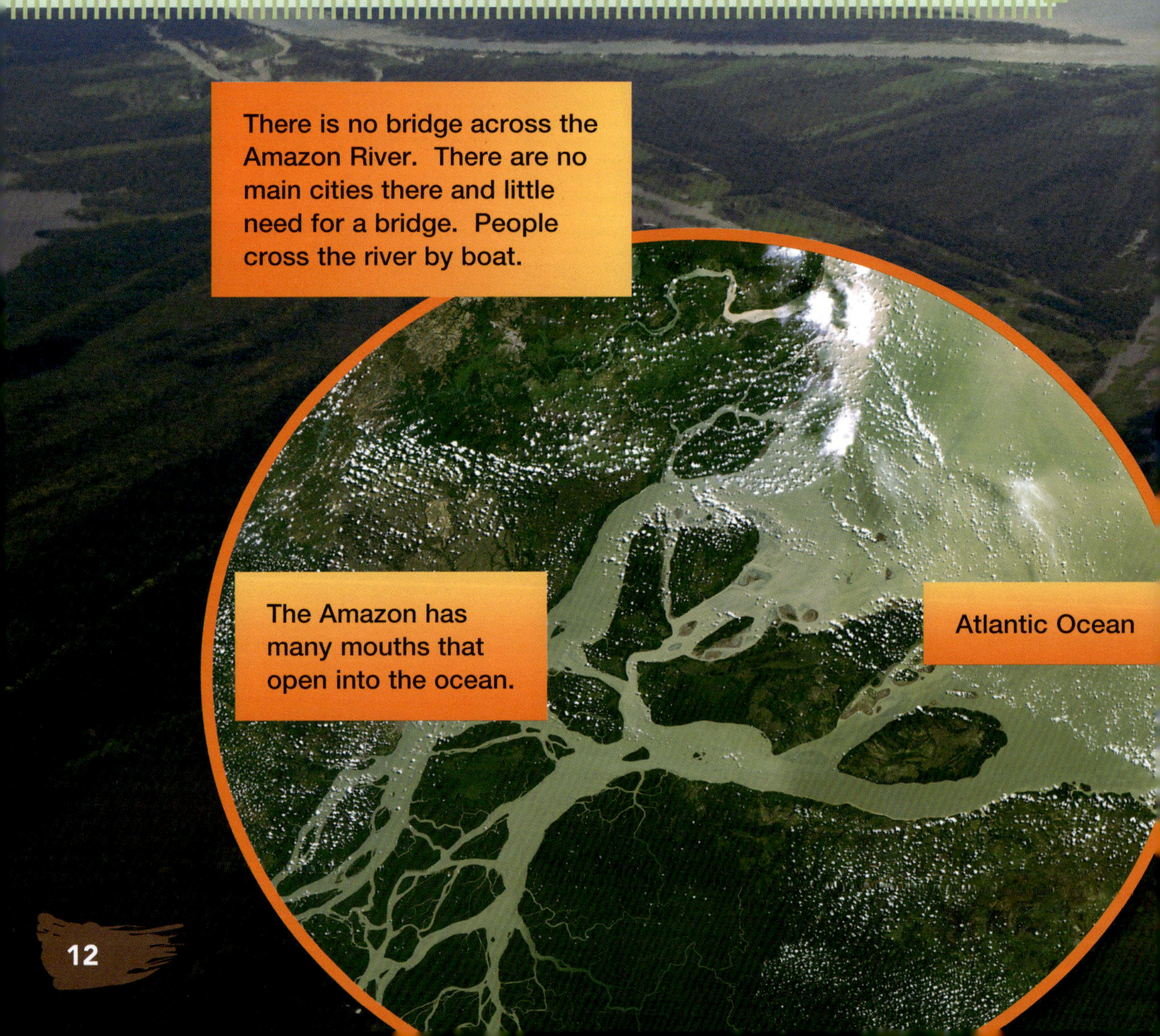

There is no bridge across the Amazon River. There are no main cities there and little need for a bridge. People cross the river by boat.

The Amazon has many mouths that open into the ocean.

The piranha is a type of fish found in the Amazon River. It is known for its sharp teeth and dangerous bite!

Amazon River

The water flowing in the Amazon River, at any given time, is more than the total water flowing in the next seven largest rivers in the world combined!

It usually rains over nine feet each year in the Amazon Rainforest.

People of the Amazon

People have been living in the Amazon for thousands of years. There are people today who live there in the same way that people long ago did. They eat food from the land and hunt. They use the trees and plants to build shelters. They try to live with the rainforest and not hurt it.

Conton, Ecuador, is a city on the edge of the rainforest.

People live in the Amazon in two very different ways.

There are also cities and towns in the rainforest. People there live in the ways that modern people do. They do not always protect the rainforest.

Descendants in the Amazon

About 500 years ago, there were millions of people in the Amazon. European explorers came and changed the people's lives. Many were killed, and even more died of European sicknesses. Just a few hundred thousand of their **descendants** live in the jungle today.

Amazon Plant Life

Step into the Amazon. You will quickly be surrounded by lush plant life. Leaves and branches tower over your head. Vines hang to the **forest floor**. Little sunlight peers through the thick tangle of trees.

The Kapok Tree

The tallest tree in the Amazon is the kapok. It can grow to 200 feet.

The kapok has lovely flowers.

You see plants and animals living in the tall branches. Their calls and chatter fill the air. This layer of trees is the **canopy**. A few trees peek up above this layer. You cannot see them from the forest floor. They are the **emergent** layer. That is because they emerge, or break through, the thick canopy.

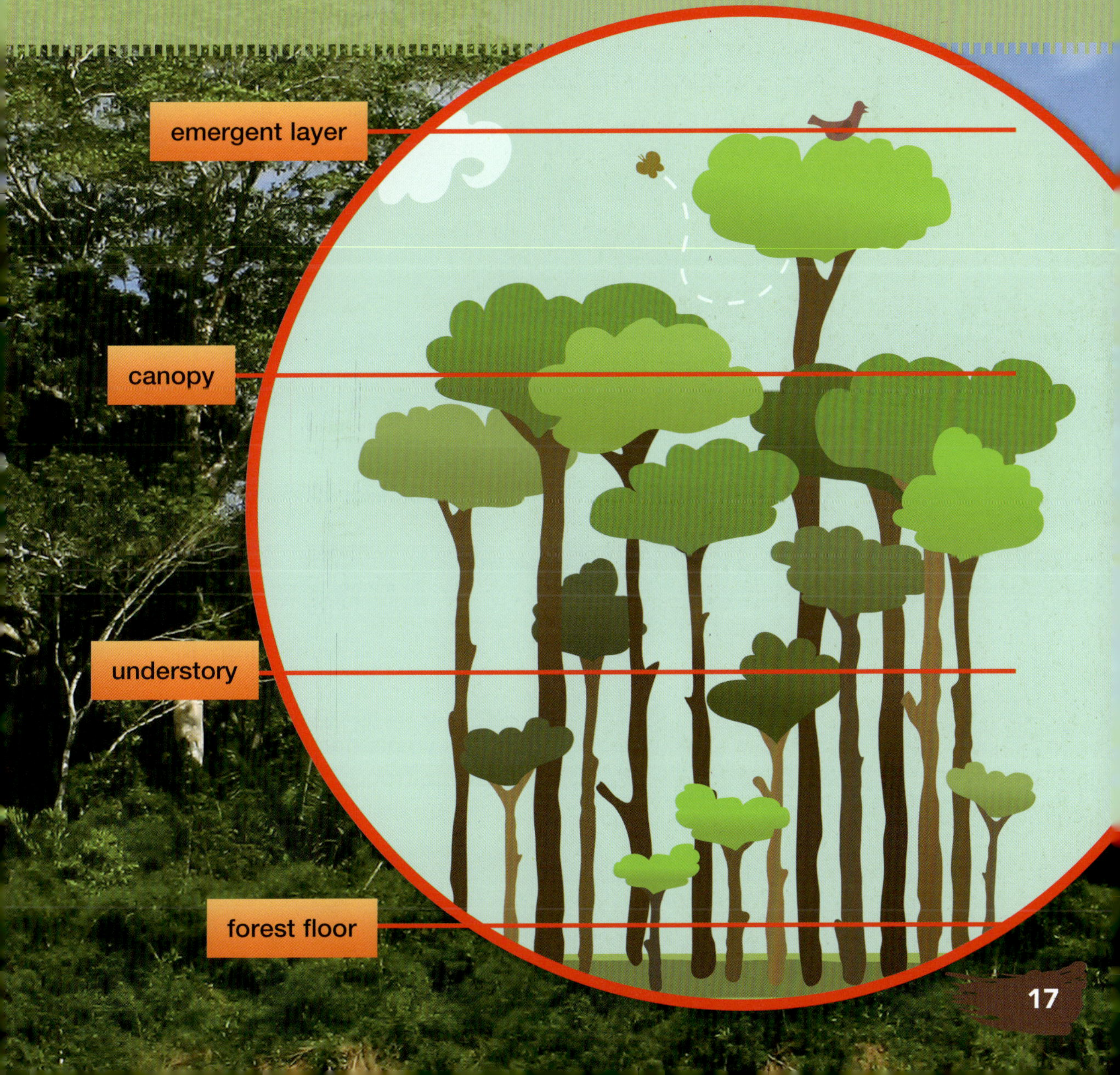

Looking down, you see the forest floor. It is covered with dead plants and even animals. They **decay**, or break down. This happens quickly because it is warm and wet.

A mushroom is the "fruit" of a fungus.

Fungus

A fungus is a living thing. It is important to a rainforest because it helps dead plants and animals decay. It uses them for food. Its waste is used by plants for food.

The **understory** is between the floor and the canopy. It is made of **shrubs** and smaller trees. Some of the small trees must wait for the older tall trees to die. Then they can grow up and take their place. Many large animals such as jaguars live in the understory. They cannot climb any higher.

Home

The rainforest floor is thick and dark. It is home to thousands of kinds of insects and small animals.

Lianas are a kind of long, woody vine. They grow in the soil but climb up trees to reach the sunlight of the canopy. Sometimes they grow between trees. Animals use them as bridges. They are even strong enough to hold people easily.

Most plants are flexible when they are young and stiff when old. Lianas are stiff when they are young and flexible when old.

Not Just for Chocolate

The cocoa tree makes more than 150 chemicals in its leaves, seeds, fruit, and bark. Native people used parts of the tree for medicine to cure coughs, fatigue, fever, and anxiety. Chocolate is also made from the cocoa tree.

Amazing Animals

You might see a paw print. You might hear the rustle of leaves. But you will never see a jaguar, unless a jaguar wants to see you—up close!

Jaguars roam the Amazon. They are powerful hunters. Native people honor the jaguar because of its power and fearlessness. It is seen as a leader and protector in the jungle. It helps to keep balance in the rainforest by hunting small **prey**.

Monkeys in the Amazon have tails that can grasp, or hold onto, objects. The tail is almost like another hand!

Big Cats

Jaguars are the third-largest feline (or cat) after lions and tigers. They can be longer than a man is tall and weigh more than a 200-pound heavyweight boxer.

One of the biggest snakes in the world is found in the Amazon. It is the green anaconda. Only one kind of snake is longer. No snake is heavier. The native people call it *mother of the waters* because it spends a lot of time in the water. Be careful if you swim in the Amazon!

An anaconda can eat large animals. It can eat a capybara (kap-uh-BAHR-uh) or even a jaguar! It catches and kills its prey by squeezing it.

The anaconda hunts at night.

Huge!

The capybara is the largest rodent in the world. It can be over 4 feet long and weigh up to 140 pounds! It lives in the Amazon and in other forest areas throughout South America.

There are thousands of insect **species** in the Amazon. We do not even know all of them. But we do know there are ants. Ants are everywhere in the jungle!

One type of ant is the army ant. These ants march in long lines like soldiers. They march to find prey. Then they swarm and eat it. They work together like a single body. They do not make noise when they march. But other animals make noise as they flee from the marching ants.

Leafcutters

Leafcutter ants get their name because they cut up plant leaves to bring back to their nests. They use the leaf bits to grow fungus, which is food for their larvae, or babies.

Toucans

One of the most unusual birds of the Amazon is the toucan. Toucans have one of the largest and most colorful **bills** of all the birds in the world.

The Future

The Amazon is full of beautiful plants and animals. Beautiful people live there, too. But there are some people who want to use the land for things that hurt the forest. They burn large areas of trees. This is called **deforestation**.

Deforestation destroys the way of life of native people. It makes thousands of animal and plant species extinct. It even changes our air and climate. The trees produce much of the air we breathe. They help to keep Earth's climate in balance.

The whole planet counts on the Amazon Rainforest. We cannot afford to lose it.

The plants of the Amazon are used for many types of medicines.

Why Deforestation?

When people clear the trees, they use the land to grow crops to feed farm animals. The farm animals feed people. It is not legal to cut the trees of the Amazon. So people burn them to hide the evidence. They destroy large parts of the rainforest every day.

Glossary

bills—large extensions from the mouths of birds, used for catching food

canopy—the uppermost parts of the trees of a forest

decay—breaking down into smaller parts through the actions of fungi, bacteria, and weather

deforestation—the cutting or burning down of plants and trees of a forest and clearing them away

descendants—all the offspring of a person or a group of people

emergent—coming through or getting a new set of characteristics

forest floor—the layer of decaying leaves and plant and animal parts on the ground of the forest

forests—thick, large areas of trees and plants

freshwater—water with very little salt, such as in lakes and streams

lianas—long, woody vines that grow from the soil to the tops of trees

prey—an animal that is hunted or captured by another animal and eaten as food

saltwater—water containing lots of salt, such as the ocean

shrubs—woody plants with branches near the ground and no main trunk

species—categories of living things, made up of related individuals

stems—the smaller sections of a river

temperate rainforest—a forest found within Earth's temperate zones, with cooler temperatures and a high amount of even rainfall

tropical rainforests—forests found within Earth's tropical zone, with higher temperatures and a high, even amount of rainfall

understory—the plants and trees of a rainforest that are below the canopy and above the forest floor; usually shaded by the canopy

Index

About the Author

William Rice grew up in Pomona, California and graduated from Idaho State University with a degree in geology. He works at a California state agency that strives to protect the quality of surface and ground water resources. Protecting and preserving the environment is important to him. He is married with two children and lives in Southern California.